short e

Sounds & Letters 2

KNOWLEDGE BOOKS

bed	red
pen	men
ten	hen
leg	

bed

③

red

pen

men

9

ten

10

hen

leg

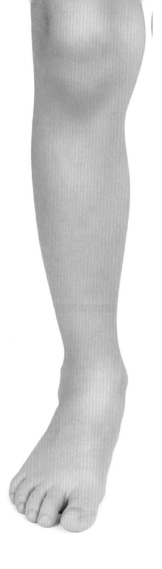

15

bed	red
pen	men
ten	hen
leg	

Knowledge Books and Software
PO Box 50 Sandgate, Queensland 4017 Australia
p. +617-55680288 f. +617-55680277 email: sales@kbs.com.au

First Published 2022
ISBN 9781922516749
Text and editing: Carole Crimeen
Design and layout: Suzanne Fletcher
Publisher: Robert Watts

Series Information: **Sounds and Letters**

Credits
Photographs: Cover © NadyaEugene; p. 1 © filuykusu, Susan Schmitz, Nattika, castiglioni veronica; p. 3 © Venus Angel; p. 7 © IB Photography; p. 9 © G-Stock Studio; p. 13 © dejavelinka; p. 15 © Purple Clouds/Shutterstock.

Phonic support books are a wonderful resource for emergent readers as they encourage independent reading and help students make the link between letters and the sounds they represent.

Have students identify the images on the title page to listen for the long or short vowel sound that they will hear through the book.

Encourage students to point to each word as they read through the book.

ISBN: 9781922516749

9 781922 516749 >

KNOWLEDGE BOOKS

Sounds &
Letters